War Poems

A Marine's Tour
2003-2008

Christopher Pascale

MERRIAM PRESS

HOOSICK FALLS, NEW YORK

2017

First Edition published in 2017 by the Merriam Press

First Edition

Copyright © 2017 by Christopher Pascale
Book design by Ray Merriam
Additional material copyright of named contributors.

All rights reserved.

The views expressed are solely those of the author.

ISBN 9781576385104
Library of Congress Control Number: 2016906022
Merriam Press #P2-P

This work was designed, produced, and published in
the United States of America by the

Merriam Press
489 South Street
Hoosick Falls NY 12090

E-mail: ray@merriam-press.com
Web site: merriam-press.com

The Merriam Press publishes new manuscripts on historical subjects, especially military history and with an emphasis on World War II, as well as reprinting previously published works, including reports, documents, manuals, articles and other materials on historical topics.

Foreword

I was a patriot, but I did not join the Marine Corps as a result of attacks on September 11, 2001, where the strike on the World Trade Center hit 30 miles west of where I grew up. I had dropped out of college shortly before this and reasoned that if I was needed, I would be drafted. No draft came, but the war in Afghanistan spilled into Iraq and I wasn't going to wait to be called the second time around, so I sent an email to both the Army and Marine Corps but did not receive a response quickly enough. On March 25, 2003 I drove to a recruiting station where I was asked to fill out a form explaining my motivations for, and expectations of, being in the Marine Corps. Among the sixteen items that I could have checked for "What I hope to gain by being a Marine" I chose the ones emboldened:

- Challenge
- Pride of Belonging
- Self-Reliance
- **Self-Discipline**
- Self-Direction
- Courage
- Poise
- Self-Confidence
- Professional Development
- **Leadership and Management Skills**
- Physical Fitness
- Technical Skills
- Travel and Adventure
- Educational Opportunity
- Financial Security
- Advancement & Benefits

And then I was asked to complete a brief narrative. I wrote the following:

> I believe it is the responsibility of a man who appreciates the opportunities his country affords him to defend it if he wishes to continue taking advantage of those opportunities in the future.

And this is the greatest loss of these wars: wasted talent. I would have joined the military at any time in my life for the opportunity to pay tribute to all of my freedoms and liberties by way of the sacrifice that comes with armed service, but only once. The war in Iraq was that one time. I, like so many men and women who served, was good at what I did; better in some areas than others and better on some days than others, fitting neatly into the machine that worked so well, but, this time, at such expense.

As you'll see in these poems, I was quite different before I joined the military (as can be expected from the age of 21 to 26). Much of the later work can be deemed as anti-war, and it is safe to say that reasonable people do not prefer war over peace, but I cannot say that the war took from me more than it gave to me. If not for it, I never would have met my wife at Keesler Air Force Base where we crossed paths on the whims of a thread so thin that it could have been broken by the slightest breeze. While I did go through periods of deep depression that led to me being suicidal, it was she who saved me. I am no longer in the military and my tendencies for suicide have subsided substantially, but I have her always.

On a personal level, I feel that I owe a debt of gratitude to the recklessness that was engaged in with these wars. But the farther I look out from my own personal benefits weighed against the overall cost, I am ashamed. I am ashamed of my own naiveté, and for the needless waste, destruction, and ignorance that came of all of this.

I served five years in the Marine Corps, starting as a Private First Class and finishing as a Sergeant. Upon graduating boot camp on Parris Island, South Carolina, I was recognized as the

Battalion Iron Man for having the highest physical fitness score out of about two-hundred-fifty. I went from never having fired a gun to being an Expert Rifleman, and had the highest qualification as a swimmer short of being an instructor, which was Water Survival Qualified (WSQ), and had been given the opportunity to go to the school for swim instruction twice, failing the indoc. the first time and then turning it down the second because I was getting out that same month and did not wish to extend my contract. I was trained as a chaser, and once used those skills to deliver a Marine to the brig. Lastly, I was a religious lay leader at the request of other Catholics in my platoon.

Upon leaving the Corps, I was offered a reenlistment bonus of $34,500, a non-deployable position at Fort Knox to be an instructor at a new school, and was encouraged to take part in a program called the Marine Corps Enlisted Commissioning Educational Program (MECEP), which would have allowed me four years to go to a university while being on active duty in exchange for four years as an officer. The money was tempting, and I did enjoy teaching, but I only wanted to join for one tour so that I could serve my country. The MECEP program was a great opportunity, but I realized that when my obligation was over I'd be 65% of the way toward retirement and my oldest daughter would be 17-years-old. It would have been foolish to get out by that time and forfeit the security of a pension, but I would have successfully denied my children the roots of a youth that included a hometown, childhood friends, and being close to relatives. On top of this, the first four years of pushing myself as hard as I possibly could had broken me. I was in constant pain and did not want to take the risk of making it permanent. Upon getting out of the military, Veterans Affairs had deemed that I was 60% disabled. What this means is that when I was leaving the military at 26, my long-term quality of life was figured to have decreased by 60% when measured to when I came in at 21.

Still, despite this, I feel richer today because of my service. Perhaps it's because my eyes have been opened. And while the light was blindingly painful to the point that I could not see that the bombs I would find on the side of the roads in Fallujah were made in America, I can see much more than that today.

—Christopher Pascale
2012

Acknowledgement

Thanks to Ray Merriam of Merriam Press. After 15 years and nearly 1,000 rejections, he's the only one who took a chance on my work.

THESE first four poems were written before I joined the Marine Corps. "The End of Summer" reflects on a life that contains real and false realities. In it, I assert that I was already a minor poet of sorts, as I supposed that I was, but also realize that certain decisions I'd made, such as leaving college to work, was foolish. It was written late one night in Long Beach, NY, after a long period of time of not writing. I had thrown my writing in the trash because I thought I'd had much of life figured out and that I wasn't going to be a writer.

Similarly, "196 Chicago Avenue" was written in a hotel room in New York. I had been having a good run with a few decent poems and holding a job, but I thought that I would have done more with my life by then, and concluded that my entire life was being wasted.

"The Deal Maker" covers the three weeks I spent as a mortgage broker. I can safely say that I was offering nothing good to society, and contributing to its ruin. I regretted leaving my job flipping burgers at Wendy's to put on a suit to do nothing, especially when I saw that it offered no value.

"The Fighting Never Ends" is a continuation of "The Deal Maker" in some ways as I compare 'middle aged men with MBAs and upside down mortgages' to 'shoemakers with bare feet.'

The End of Summer

Driving the streets drunk
in a truck like you're
on some racetrack
while you think and
those thoughts drown.

And you pull into a place

to sit down and gather
yourself; always remembering
to never start a poem
with some bullshit action
                    sentence.

The people in the place
aren't allowed where
you're allowed so they
bitch [they always bitch]
while you got those cool
cross-trainers, $150 jeans,
a $2 shirt and fleece
that you used to think
could pass for a jacket
because of all those nights
in the clubs with girls
pulling you into corners too
                    drunk to talk
while you thought you
were some kind of a big
shot with the money in
your pocket when there
was money in your pocket.
Then some girl said
        aren't you hot

        ...
        maybe you should take
                off your fleece

Slut.

Then you moved
back home and fell
apart, throwing your second
novel and three books of poems
in the trash – fucking

big shot – and now you're
drunk and the coffee won't
change that.

You're not too sure about
a lot of things, but
you've always been willing
to the possibility that everything
you've been doing is completely
                              wrong,
and as you get back
in that rocket, balls
full of vodka and sperm,
there's going to be another
        Got Jesus
billboard along the nude beach
while the kids are parked
in their cars underneath
screwing to rap music.

Where'd the term screwing
come from? It's really
more like a hinge than
a screw.

And you think of that
kid who put a file in that
girl that time. What was
he thinking? It was a
first date. People don't
seem to realize that after
a month you can pretty
much get away with anything
so long as you can back
it up with some kind of
article or website (you can
make the website) especially

if the two of you are
1) very insecure
2) bad conversationalists
                or
3) selfish
and you can rest assured
when it comes to your
sex life because most people
are all three.

The feelings wear off
and now that most of
the bullshit is flaked off
your brain you can
finally ask yourself what
the hell you're doing
in this dude's house, drinking
the coffee his wife made
while he's at work and
she's making sure the
kids don't wake up,
thinking you might stick
it to her when you'd
sooner give it to an
electrical socket all sopped
up with baby oil.

You get up and drive into
Long Beach (NY) to an
apartment building, leave
an old book at a door
where you had a business
meeting where there was a
ten minute discussion of
the irrelevance between
happiness and money, then
he said, 'I wouldn't be

happy making that much
money,' and you left
shortly after he bitched
about being a math teacher,
and how since he can't make
it as a poet, then no one can.

After the meeting was
over his friend (and yours)
asked, "why didn't you tell
him who you were?"
but you didn't answer.
You didn't answer.

196 Chicago Ave.

The plane flies in and
they make us wait and wait,
and then we get to go. The
hotel is close but I have
to wait and wait, and then
go. The room is just a
room and I don't have
anything to do until tomorrow
so I sit and sleep and
drink and stare out at the
street from a chair as the
cars go by.

I wonder if everyone else
was so ideal when they
were poor. I was going to
have children, teach children, be
noticeably influential in this century,
but here I am with the
chance, and all I'm going to do
tonight is play Sim City on

the big screen TV, drink a
bottle of Bourbon, and masturbate
in the window with the light-
switch flipping on and off.

The TV is on and an evangelist
is saying he'll give 10% of
your donation to God. That's
real swell of him. Maybe I'll
put $10 on my Visa card so
I can be a buck more in
favor of the Big Guy, and
maybe be overlooked for all
of the things I won't do tonight.

The Deal Maker

These houses all start to
blend together after a while.
First it was the phone
numbers, then the faces. Now
everything is consolidated.

I pull up in my clean
car, a white Honda, and
my blue tie so I
don't remind them of a
                    banker.

I pass a black
pick-up truck with dirt
all over the front and the
word DICKFOR smeared
across the hood. I ring the
bell with a smile that
would finish off a coma
patient, and think, yeah,

keep smiling, jerkoff.

We consolidate their credit cards
into the mortgage. Now they
owe $15,000 more on the house
than they paid so we celebrate
by cutting up two of their
six cards as they talk
about a wedding and an
antique auction. The papers are
signed and they thank me
as I leave.
"Thank you so much," he
says with a hardy handshake.
"Thanks a lot," she says.

I leave.

Their son was pushing his
skateboard around the drive-
way as I got into my car
and I said, "hey."
"You talking to me?"
"Yeah."
"What?"
I pointed to the hood and asked,
"What's a dickfor?"

He cracked up as I drove
away, and I just kept
thinking, *keep laughing, kid. It's
the only thing your parents
are going to leave you.*

The Fighting Never Ends

It's 6:00 on a Friday
night. The Sun's already
gone; hanging out there in
California blanketing the
graveyards while the people
in China are working their
asses off and starving
almost to death, but not quite.

The businessmen are driving
home in their leased autos –
middle aged men with MBAs
and upside down mortgages –
like shoe makers with bare feet.

Where does love go when the
war's over? I haven't eaten
anything but pussy in the
past six days; dirty hooker
snatch gets the jaw strong
they say
like a mouthful of razorblades, or
having a mother-in-law who
hates you for no reason at all.

In 5,000 years the Muslim race
will dominate and the Hasidic
Jews will have reservations with
retail prices, and that's a
real shame because the Jews
truly could've made a comeback
had they not let their temples
go to waste with majority leadership.

The American Empire
will be gone as well,
and reduced to a sub-
chapter in the history books
if they still have books in
5,000 years. And someone
will be weak and someone
will be strong, but they can't
beat us all.

The divorce rate will make
a comeback from its
downward cycle into the
eighties, but then go back
down (like I did to your mother
last night) because they can't
get us all. Even your
mother can't get us all.

THE following three poems would not be considered war poems, but they were written in response to my girlfriend breaking up with me while I was in basic training, and then again when I came home. I tried to make it through with humor, but in the end was just sad to have lost her.

Love Lost

So here we go again;
another one gone.

And it's always the same.
Women are great at
the game of love, but even better
with their excuses.

It's always
you treat me like a prostitute
or
you make me feel like a whore
or
why are you leaving forty dollars on the nightstand?

Not once has a woman just
come out and said that she
doesn't like me for me.

The phone rings. It's Monica.
I better get to an ATM.

Autumn

Autumn is here, dark and brown and orange
as it settles into the winter of my heart.
The leaves pile up outside, the house is
a mess and it's time for me to leave.

Autumn is here and this has been a mistake
for both of us to go as far as we did,
but sometimes it's hard to tell how far
we're supposed to go; how far not to go.

Autumn, it is time for you to leave. This
has been a mistake. But this must be why
pencils were given erasers; not so much
because our relationship can be fixed, but
because you're such a damn slut that you
probably make a lot of mistakes when you
                              write shit down, too.

Chanelle

There's a spider crawling across
from me. In his world he's
huge, and I'm far away.

The sky flashes with heat and light
as I think of how I could have
run faster that day in boot camp
but didn't give a shit. I was
through impressing them. I was
done putting out and taking crap
when I could just take crap
all by itself. I missed you.

I reach my hand out and slap
at the spider. Dead.

I'm a killer. That's what I do.

I think about playing the piano
instead of throwing it out. It
brought me closer to God as I
centered myself in the universe,
and I needed a safe distance.
I was never good enough anyway.

The world will do without me and
my piano, but there are things
I have to do before I die; things
I have to suffer through as I
think of you, how close we'd be. You
were right there and now you're
gone. I guess I miss you, but
you're somewhere else right now
as I think of you and how you
wouldn't reach me if you knew how,
and how I wouldn't know how to
                          if I could.

And I think of you.
But you're not thinking of me.

FOLLOWING basic training, I was on 10 days of leave prior to going to combat training at the School of Infantry. As I was waiting to go, I sat in my childhood bedroom recovering from the injuries I'd incurred that included rashes and a numbness in my toes and hip from the strain of wearing boots most of the day and the weight of a cartridge belt.

The Champ

There's a war in Africa. I'm
on Long Island with my orders.

    Camp Lejeune, NC

I beat the system for a little
while, but tomorrow I'll have
my combat boots on as they
hike us out into the field
and we play soldier with our
empty rifles and loaded peckers.
In boot camp they gave us a
shot with some kind of no-
boner serum. It was kind of nice,
but here, no shot.

Out in the field your energy is like
a river; not endless, but enough,
and when you get out your
body is all messed up.
It's fucking awful.
I have no feeling in most of my
toes, but the feeling's not lost.

Most of it has gone to my penis
that was once flaccid and serum-
filled, but is now mighty and
powerful. Small villages could be
plundered with one swoop of my
huge and great cock. Their women would
all suffer my wrath for no
rubber could prevent my well trained
and complacent sperm as the
muscles would shoot the hot streams
through the weak latex,
nullifying all spermicide,
bypassing her egg as they pierce
the ovary and puncture the lung;
only one lung.

But it's like my dad used to say on Sunday
mornings when he cooked us kids eggs
and mom slept until noon. Dad
always said, *you gotta pay the
price if you wanna go a few
rounds with the champ.*

MY father had never served in the military (his draft number for Vietnam was 356) and the first time I ever went camping was in boot camp, so this poem is purely fiction, but the nightmares I had learned about that other veterans had had inspired this, and I wondered if I would make such a mistake as the one "Dad" had that would haunt me the rest of my life.

Camping With Dad

When I was seven my dad
took me camping out in
New Jersey. Wildwood.

We hiked the campground and
dad taught me how to use a
compass. He said, *you'll
never actually need to know
how to use this, but it's interesting
to see how far we've come
from where we were.*

We had dinner and then
I played with dad's lighter
until the fluid was gone.

But at night the fun was
over. Dad woke me up
tap tap tap
tap tap tap
on the bottom of my foot.
John, he said, *John, wake up.*

My name isn't John.
I was awake.

John, he said trying to
light his lighter *John, listen –*
it wouldn't light – *Fuck,*
man, I'm sorry. I left
my rifle outside. I need you
to come with me to find it.
I think I left it by the
tree I pissed on. John…
JOHN, are you listening to me?
Are you fucking listening!

He shook me hard and saw he
wasn't where he thought he was.
Neither of us slept the rest of
the night.

At dawn we drove home.
Four hours. No words.
We never went camping again.

I couldn't understand
what had happened to Dad.
I was only seven.
I had never been to the
jungles of Columbia.
I had never been to the
cities in Africa.
I had never been to the
desert.

I had never had
someone shoot at me, miss
and I shot them only to
have their thirteen year old

son pick up the gun [some-
day my son would be thirteen]
and take aim as my rifle
jammed from ten feet away,
so I stuck him in the
throat with my knife
and kicked off it,
never pausing. And a month
later get my best friend
killed because I left my weapon
leaning against a tree with the
butt stock in a puddle of piss
and flies.

I couldn't understand
what had happened to Dad.
I was only seven.

WATCHING the news one night, there was another scandal about Michael Jackson, the singer, and his sleepovers with young boys. As I watched the talking heads and TV show host, there was a ticker going by on the bottom of the screen. The old news of two dead Americans in the war was cited as a footnote for the day. Sometime after this, I remember there was day-long news coverage about the late actor, John Belushi, which included numerous interviews with his widow. As a nation, we were getting a little bored with the wars. It was 2004.

The Good Fight

Two soldiers died in Iraq today.
I flipped on the television and there it was;
a byline underneath the real story:
Michael Jackson. Did he do it or not?
Everybody thinks so, and the coverage
will continue for at least a week as we
wonder where the truth really lies.
And what the hell is wrong with him?
What's wrong with him.
Right.

Last night it was, 'hey, that Michael Jackson thing
is on TV.' Then tomorrow it'll be, 'did you see that
Michael Jackson thing?' after a joke about the
janitor who sat in on a confessional in place of
the priest and asked the altar boy what Father
Mike gave for oral sex, after hearing a woman's
confession. Then the altar boy said,
"twenty bucks."

And we wonder
what the hell is wrong with them.

Two soldiers died in Iraq, and there it was, a
testimony to what we love, a picture of Skeletor,
the greatest pop sensation of the 20th century
and a fan calling in telling Michael to fight
the good fight
as soldiers die in Iraq,
or so the blurb said.
It was more of a passing byline, really.

FAITH is an important part of many people's lives in the military. In basic training, church allowed us to escape our drill instructors. Out of habit, some of us continued to go who hadn't gone before. Before my faith in those who ran the United States began to fade, I was struggling with those who ran the Catholic Church. I recall that in 2004 a newspaper article had been released stating that Pope John Paul II was discussing the great wrongs that were going on in the church. Among them was that lay people had sometimes led services, and not among them was the rampant abuse by the church leadership, which included stealing children from single mothers and selling them in Spain years before, and numerous cases of rape and sexual assault on young children much more recently. Priests who stole money from the church were being publicly excommunicated, and those who stole everything from a child were being secretly hidden away. While this is not related to the war, it does pertain to my early enlistment.

The Dark Room

I've heard that there are notes
that will please the Lord
but music never entered such
rooms as my mind, for it is
a room where shelves lay bare
and there is no consent.

Where boys kneel before altars in
churches, are told to be good for
God. God wants them to be
Good...to be silent, for silence
is the mystic ram.

The altar bleeds like the believer
does when faith knifes his back, and
he cries like we cry when the
only thing we believe in has
been stolen from us.

The door closes. It closes
quietly as the wards of God's
men say to walk and live
forgivingly. No one can beat a
faithful man and get away with it,
and that may be why their faith
is stolen from them in dark
rooms with holy novelties
by their salesmen.

All those years of sacrifice
are gone after one big party
and a life of sin granting a
destiny for Hell as they pass
it all through the counterpart
that gives me a life of
guilt and mistrust, destined for
Hell myself, so I can see
them again and kill them.

The door closes quietly
as the silence enrages
through quiet contempt in a
room of sin; a life of sin,
and the light that never
comes. It never comes.

For God does not love me. God
cannot love me. Like the
light that never comes
so is He.

I wrote this as a sixth verse to the song of the same title, and just as other songs with an extra verse added (Amazing Grace being one) it has no place being sung in addition to the performance of the original.

Hallelujah

Two friends
they walk alone
hand and hand
on the broken road.
Their people are very proud.
Hallelujah.

Then a thrown stone
hit the wall,
and Mohammed
began to fall.
Oh, how Jesus must be proud.
Hallelujah.
Hallelujah.
Hallelujah.

June in Kuwait

Death in peace keeping, but who
really cares if you're some poor
son-of-a-bitch making less than
minimum wage trying to keep
the peace and no one understands?

Somewhere in the states there's
a single mom, and her only
little boy is over there being
threatened everyday
wondering if he'll make it home.

He won't.
They'll send a letter and
the insurance company is going
to try and screw her out
of the $250,000 policy
he bought, and they won't
have to try very hard
because she doesn't want
any money.
She wants her little boy.

She'll hold his picture and
cry. She'll cry because
this world is built on
dreams, and dreams die.
But she didn't know that.

A Gay Experience

When I was a kid we
used to play a game called
'kill the man with the ball'
before the mommies and
daddies got a hold of
it; the same game they
played as kids, only they
called it 'smear the queer.'

But you can't say queer
anymore if you want to lace
up a pair of tan suede
boots with an M16 over
your shoulder and 180
rounds on your back
to play hide 'n seek
with a bunch of Arabs.
No, you have to say
homosexual
or strange.

For instance, say you're
at a party and you see
a gay
that's right,
a gay
you couldn't just say 'that guy's
kinda faggy;' you'd have
to proceed with extreme
caution to your nearest
friends and say,
"Hey Bob, is that
guy...you know...
strange?"
"Oh yeah, he's *really* strange."

Before you know it I'll be
starting sentences that begin
with *before long* instead,
and Tom Petty's song,
"Don't do me Like That"
will become a song we all
love hearing. The video stores
will have a strange section,
and my son will ask if
we can rent Smashed up From
the Ass up 5, a family favorite
starring Ron Bondem, and I'll
say, 'we just rented that last week!
Mom loved it. Of course
we'll rent it again,'
as I recall how merry
and gay that evening was.

But, eventually, it'll get to the
point where we can't even have a
gay experience with our children.
The world will be too strange.
The new craze will be moving
forward, and if you're not moving
forward you're standing still. Add
inflation and you're fucked, but
we can't say fucked, so we
can't get fucked, and state laws
say some funny things about
sodomy, so blow jobs are out
of the question, too, and that really
sucks, but at the same time
it doesn't. And
it just goes on and on.

THERE is one battle from the Korean War all marines are taught about in basic training, the Battle of the Chosin Reservoir. We learned that the infantry units had been devastated by the outnumbering attacking forces and that all who were left were the cooks and desk jockeys. Since every marine is a rifleman, the incoming forces were held off for seventeen days. The defending unit had nowhere to retreat, insufficient clothing for the weather, and no way of knowing if they would live or die.

During the more recent wars, it was well known that some young (and not-so-young) women were making it clear that they were home alone, but didn't want to be. Among the signs left out were trashcans turned upside down and a certain color porch light. While many used these signs as a means of solidarity with neighbors who were also alone, others were more adventurous.

The Frozen Chosen

It's frozen in the desert
tonight. 30 degrees before sunrise,
80 in the day, and I'm
shivering on my watch in
a hole. How does it feel
to dig your own grave?
they say. Not so bad.
Not so bad.

Back home the wives of
deployed men leave blue porch
lights on so other people
know they're lonely, and
maybe they can cure them

of their blue lights.

Some of us lie to ourselves,
imagining it's just other
lonely wives coming over
with their kids. They put a
video in for the children
as they drink lemonade or
vodka or both on the back
porch while Dora the
Explorer is playing in
the background, and they laugh
about things to pass the time.

But that's not true, and I
know that. We all know
that, and as I fight the impending
sleep that tries to overcome me,
hoping I won't have to pull
this trigger as I hallucinate and
shake from a fever as I freeze
out in the desert in the
30-degree cold, I know that
some asshole is inviting
himself into my house with
a twelve pack of condoms
and a six pack of beer.
But my wife doesn't drink beer,
and as she looks at him
she'll think of me, realizing
that she can do much better
than a fuck-head like him.
As he leaves he'll see the
street I live on ablaze
with blue porch lights:
the gold rush of
North Carolina.

It's freezing out here
tonight and when my
watch is over I'll
crawl into my
sleeping bag trying
to get warm next to a
rebel flag toting son-
of-a-bitch that would
die for me out here in
the desert, but back in
the states tell me that
if the north is so
great maybe I should
stay there. Maybe I should.

It's freezing out tonight, and
I die a little more every
day as I wonder if I
can finish my watch;
if I'll make it home,
and if I do, what'll be
there?
Because I know my wife
leaves the porch light on.
I just don't know if
it's for me.

I never did any Pacific tours. But I'd heard some stories from those who had.

The Roosevelt List

It's cold again tonight.
Cold and sick.
I think of being
back in the Philippines
where the whores are
as common as herpes
and as expensive as
candy bars.

We were there for seven
days and drank and played
pool in the bars where
we talked to the women—
women who hated us, but not
our money—and I sat
with my back to the stage
and wondered why there were
so many prostitutes on
this beautiful island as I
bought another round for
Sally and slid my hand
a little higher.

Later that night, after
what was (for me) a
nice and cheap evening,

she started talking. I
wanted to leave, but it
was my room. I shouldn't
have to leave. She should.
Why was she talking anyway?
I didn't care about her or her
family. I'm an American.
Americans don't care.
We're just nosey bitches
with long pointing fingers.
I must've made her come
or something. You make
a woman spill a little, and
they just dump the rest
out. They're funny like that.

Somewhere in Saigon Sally's words
I heard her say something
about Teddy Roosevelt. I
took the pillow off
my head and rolled over.

Damn right he was badass,
I said.
*Did you know that when he
got the call to be President
he was climbing a mountain?
He had asthma, too. A lot
of people don't know that.*

Then she said that he was
a bad man, and I went
back to the pillow as she
went on about 1904, 'a great
day in American history,' T.R.
said, as thousands of boys
came home in their US

Army outfits after a one
month killing spree in the
Philippines. 250,000 dead.
But war is hell,
and on P.I. in 1904
so was peace.

My mind began to drift
again, but to the first grade.
My best friend was Filipino.
His older brother taught me
how to play baseball.
They should have been there
that night to help me out of
this but they weren't,
and she wasn't going to
just shut up so I
reached into my shoe and
pulled another $5 from
my wallet and fell asleep
while she went down on me
just as I'm sure
someone did to big Ted
when he climbed off that
mountain and into that
comfy chair in the Oval
Office before he added all
those names to his list.

MANY days are missed with family. During my time in Iraq I missed my wife's and daughter's birthdays, and the birth of my second child. My wife had sent a Red Cross message, but the doctor noted that a Cesarean Section surgery (major surgery) posed a low risk of death, so my unit denied me from going home after allowing my squad leader to do so for the same reason. I don't believe they were favoring him or punishing me; I just think his wife had a better doctor who explained that a woman should not even drive a car for two weeks much less care for a household. Later, I found out that the doctors thought she was going to die as they could not bring her out of unconsciousness.

This poem is about my wife and our family with references to me trying to find success while clinging to the inspiration of others as I could not seem to attain it.

The Biography Section

Don't send me anything for my
birthday, she said,
while I'm here in Iraq.
Back home we qualify for
welfare, WIC and food stamps.
My wife is pregnant and sick,
and I'm here.
Don't get me anything for my
birthday, she said.

But we're used to getting by.
Before I came here I'd made
$14,000. $6,000 for car insurance,
$3,000 for rent, and nothing left over.

She's twenty-one.
I try to remember my twenty-
first birthday. I was in
Massachusetts in a one bedroom
suite with my girlfriend.
One month later I was on
Parris Island. She sent me one
of those letters, and I can't
blame her. Eating pussy takes
confidence and I didn't have
it; not until I went to Texas
to visit my wife a year later,
determined to make this work.

My wife is an amazing
woman. At sixteen, a high school
dropout after two years of being
labeled a retard she was
flipping burgers, married
and pregnant. She convinced her
neighbor down the street to teach her
to be a brick mason.
I'll never be late for work,
she said. *I don't have a*
car. Meanwhile, she turned her
house into a bed and breakfast while
her husband stopped working because
philandering was too much as it was,
and she was too blind to notice,
but after a year it was hard to miss.
Get a job or get out, she said.
I can't take care of the three
of us alone, so he took the
money for the baby's furniture,
bought a second car, and left.

Then she married me, sold her

house, and put the money away
for our daughter's college. Today
it would cover a year's tuition.
Tomorrow, a year's books.

One less thing.

*Don't get me anything for my
birthday*, she said.

I've read five books since I
left to keep feeding my mind.
It's either active or dormant, a
good friend told me, *and a
dormant mind can't win the war.*

I've written two books out
here because that same friend
told me *write like hell*; to write
until there's nothing left, and then
dig a little deeper to finally scratch
the surface of what you're capable
of. He said writing is hard, but
not as hard as not writing so
struggle because the struggle makes
you strong. I took his word for
it because a man in his eighties,
a former Army Captain—Jewish—
who landed on Normandy before taking
his platoon into Germany where they
tore down a billboard that said,

> Give me ten years and
> you won't recognize Germany

that was signed by Adolf Hitler (and
he was right) might just know. He led

his platoon to a work camp, shut it down,
and went home. The war was over,
but his hatred for what had happened
still lives today.

The road has been paved by
men far greater than me,
yet I struggle where they
made it easy. They all told me
that you have to be willing
to lose again and again and again,
because that's what they did.
I lose and feel like a loser.
Do it again, they say,
and again and again and again.
I do. I lose.
Do it again.
I do it again.
Do it again.
I do it again.
Do it again.
And my mother asks, *how
much rejection are you going to
take?* And I don't know
as her heart breaks for me and
my family while I tell my
wife we will not accept any
subsidies as I would wake
at 4AM, get home whenever,
eat, write, lay my head down
at midnight. *What are your
dreams* I once asked her, and
fell asleep no sooner than she
started to tell me.

Senator John McCain vacationed at
the Hanoi Hilton, and years later

lost his run at the presidency but
not his balls. He was the first one
to call out George W. Bush on Iraq,
and the first one to call out John
Kerry when he was full of shit.
And my wife wrote a letter to
me. It said this:
Don't get me anything for my
birthday.
It said it several times.

EVEN in the middle of a mission, there's downtime. Sometimes you sit by yourself and a memory is triggered about something that is buried deep enough that it almost never surfaces. Some of the memories are those of regret; others are sad. When I wrote this, remembering the overconfident kid I had been, we were at a water treatment plant, or something of the like. A reserve unit was guarding it, making it a safe place to sleep for a few nights while we were on a mission. I was attached to a recon team from 1st platoon, Alpha Company out of Okinawa, Japan as one of two engineers. We were on standby in the event that any of the commandos who were working in pairs or alone in the city of Falluja needed immediate assistance. Having time to think and read, I did.

High School Swim Practice

Sitting here under the Sun
with a cigar
I hit the button on the
lighter, watch the leaves catch
the flame and suck in a
mouthful of smoke that resonates
of burnt coffee,
which is better than no coffee,
I guess.

It takes me back to
high school swim practice.
I'd swim a few laps and
stare at my coach's legs, well,
not her legs exactly.
Swim! She'd say,

and I'd haul ass through the
next part of the workout so
I could hang on the lane again,
enamored by the six-foot-tall,
beach volleyball-playing goddess
that stood over us with
bronzed blonde hair and skin
to match.

The fathers never missed a meet.
No one ever missed practice either, or
the bus ride there where she'd
sit with us while we told her
dirty jokes and she talked to
me about art and poetry;
her boyfriend and college as
I eased my way into the
seat beside her.

Halfway through the season I came
home from a ski trip with
my girlfriend. 'How was it,'
she asked. I told her it
was a good workout and she said,
'I bet it was,' with a slight
smile as her eyes said
I bet you could fuck like crazy,
because I could.

The season ended and I pulled
her in the pool with me with
all her clothes on, and when we
surfaced she threw her hair
back and smiled like
she could've kissed me as
the rest of the guys jumped in.

The last trip back I sat in
the back seat staring out the
window, depressed, knowing I'd
never see her again to
go swimming at the beach
where she lived alone in a
tiny apartment. I imagined
us fucking like crazed animals
and driving up and down the
coast in some convertible car I
didn't own. We'd vacation on the
outskirts of beautiful cities, see
an opera, go to museums and the
track where we'd watch the athletic
animals pound through the dirt.
Late at night we'd smoke a
cigar out on the balcony of
one of our cottages. I'd pick
her up, light as a feather,
as the moon made the sky
seem like day, take her to
bed, and make love to her
all night.

I had forgotten about these
things for so long until my
wife put the picture of the
swim team over our fireplace, and
I saw her again standing right
next to me.
I told K the stories and
she said that I probably could've
had her, but I said that
I wouldn't have even if I
could because I could never respect
a woman who would sleep with me.

DURING a patrol I was with a fire team of marines and we had to cross a rivulet with bamboo shoots coming out of it. Everyone made it across easily, but I had somehow fallen through to my hips. It was July 30, 2005 and the weather was about 140 degrees. I handed over my gear, pushed myself up and continued on, heavier with the weight of the water in my trousers and boots. We had just begun our patrol and this had made it much longer. As I struggled, I dug deep as I had learned to do over the recent years. I searched for the motivation that would push me forward and in it I concluded that I had to finish this patrol because I wanted to be what I believed I was: the best. Coming back from it hours later, I sat alone going through the contents of my wallet, finding the picture of my oldest daughter and the sonogram of my youngest still intact with my money and other things. The following poem is not true in that I relied on Scott Goodman to get me through this trial, but it is true that he was a good man, and I cannot honestly say why I was thinking of him in the state that I was; perhaps it was because he was with me in my time of need.

Conversations With Scott Goodman

Scott Goodman was a good man.

I only knew him in the last
years of his life when cancer
was winning the war within.

He tried to be my friend, but
I did my best to stay away
from him as I hid in his
daughter's bed █████████

████████████ while she
██████████.
But some moments
I couldn't escape.

He took me to lunch
and asked,
what do you want out
of life, Chris?
And I told him of my
dreams, and then
discounted them.

It was the only conversation
we had ever had and
it ended with him telling
me that if I ever spoke
like that again I would
not be allowed to
see his daughter.

Following that he lost his
ability to speak and died
unable to eat or shit
on his own, but instead, in
the presence of his daughter
and a wife who he married
again so he could give her
more money rather than pay
it away in taxes; a humiliating
end to a great life.
I was fifteen.

The years passed and
I dropped his daughter
but still talked to him
as I left the Division

I college that paid me
a tiny scholarship to
swim and dive in their
pool, saying,
I gotta do this, Scott.
I'm too old to play kids'
games and write silly
papers for free.

He told me I was doing
the right thing and
I realized I never
asked him if he had
ever gone to college. It was
his daughter who told me
about him becoming an
insurance salesman after
the military, going on to
own his own company which
he sold and stayed on at
until his death.
You're doing the right
thing, he said, *if*
you actually do it.
And I tried,
failing miserably through
the best days of my life
as I'd talk to him in my
car about girls and money,
and he kept me strong.

When CNN and Fox News kept
showing segments of Iraq
and Afghanistan all day
I told him before anyone,
I have to do this,
and he said the same

words my father did;
do it only if you think
it's the right thing to
do as my mother cried.

And today, as the Sun
scorched my boots and
blouse, drying them within
ten minutes of me falling
into a stagnant bog, I
told him that I didn't
know if I could make it.
Help me, I said,
I need you.
And he said,
you don't need me.
Everything you need is
already inside of you.
Now take yourself home.

And I did.

LOVE poems are a funny thing, and, normally, rejected poems never earn a response, but I received a phone call regarding this one. The call was from the woman who had reviewed it. She told me that she had liked it very much, but that this poem about me loving my wife and missing her while I was deployed was not going to be allowed into the *Coastal Carolina Community College Anthology* alongside such works as the many ENG101 essays since the backdrop of the narrative is that of me attempting to masturbate in a shower, and failing. Perhaps if I had come gloriously it would have made the difference, but I didn't, so it didn't.

For K

It was a lonely night
in Mississippi outside of
that movie theater where you
found me with some other
woman.
We spent the night
with you telling me
about your love of
Charles Dickens.
I think I was in love
with you already.
Hurt and in love.

Of all the low lives
you could have walked into
you found mine,
and saved it.

I flip through the pages
of a Victoria's Secret
10,000 miles away uninspired,
unsure of whether it's from
the four scoops of ice
cream every day,
bags of potato chips,
or the happy marriage
you've given me
that has sunken my libido
so low that it causes me to
stop in the shower as
I approach climax for no
reason other than that I
don't give a shit as I attempt
to get myself there with
thoughts of someone else,
but nothing works:
like life before I met you
when it was nothing more
than a barren wasteland;
a bath to wallow in the despair.

Then you were there
with the fruits of a
world not meant for me,
saving my life
and making it yours.

FINANCES are a common hardship for young families in the military. When my wife and I married I was a Lance Corporal. We had a child already, and then our second was born around the time I became a Corporal. As mentioned earlier, we qualified for multiple forms of assistance and I was too stubborn to accept that if I received a federal salary and qualified for federal assistance, then it stood to reason that that assistance was part of my pay. Instead, I felt like a failure, ashamed that I was unable to give my family a nice life and fulfill the promises I had made to them. The film, "Cinderella Man," starring Russell Crowe as James Braddock, the boxer, had come out, and it lead to me writing this poem while trying to find a second job so that my wife could take courses at the community college and we could pay off our credit card.

Jimmy Braddock

I was looking through the want
ads and they said:

WANTED
Highly trained professional.
Regular pay, long hours, welfare.
Uncle Sam wants you.

But they say that Jimmy
Braddock collected a welfare
check—it was cash back
then—before he became the
heavyweight champ, built a
heavy equipment company,
and served honorably in WWII.

It was the depression and he
found regular work but couldn't
pay his bills while his wife
sliced each piece of salami as
thin as she could so it'd
last just a little longer.

Here I've got food for a
week, a government house
I could never afford on
what I make, and two kids.
I wake up in the morning
driven and that drive
saps away into the nether
regions of nowhere as I sit
in traffic praying that a
drunk driver will crush my
1990 powder blue Plymouth
as the gas tank is blissfully
full for that perfect
moment of impact.
But it hasn't happened yet.

I come home both dead
and alive to a wife who
wants to go to college;
wants to get a job;
wishes she'd never
married me.

I clean a room in the house,
mow the yard;
do anything to feel like
I'm doing something since
I can't take care of my family.

I lay my head down at

night waking with the drive
that gets me into my car
and realize that I'm just
like Jimmy Braddock,
except Jimmy Braddock
didn't suck.

THIS poem is about Richard Dudas, a professional baseball player who served as a fighter pilot in Vietnam.

600 Feet Over Hanoi

He tasted death a mile high
tanked on adrenaline, fear,
and hopes that he would go home,
or not, as he closed the cockpit and
the afterburners streaked through
the Viet Cong sky while
lead and acid rained down on
the black, white, and brown boys
on the ground.

Back home, Thurmon Munson
was no longer in the Ohio League
where they once rivaled each
other. He was in Brooklyn
getting dressed in the same
locker room Lou Gehrig
and Babe Ruth once had;
going out for a recreational drink or
two after practice, screwing
groupies and going back to work,
never thinking of that fighter
pilot who was just on a long
list of ball players that had
failed against him to steal
second, earning him his day in
the Sun as he made it to

that cathedral called
Yankee Stadium.

Dick finished his tour having
lost both his roommates;
one a vapor of pink mist
in that God-forsaken sky,
the other a tortured prisoner
in Hanoi. He signed his papers
and went right back knowing
he would die – hoping he would die.

'Some men get to roll the
dice their whole life,' he
said, 'but a man like me has
already had more than his
fair share.'
It was time to go home.
But the war ended.

Back home he was a baby
killer, a scumbag, a
fucking fascist, and
hippies were all the rage
with their multi-colored
vans and the violent protests
nobody remembers while the
WWII vets were too busy thinking
of themselves to do a damn
thing for anyone else.

It was a crazy time, and
Dick sat at home while
TV told him to wear bell
bottom pants and shirts
with flowers as his son
watched him stare down the bottom

of every bottle, wondering
which one would kill him.
Then he changed the scenery
and eyed the barrel of his
pistol while the small
child at his feet watched him
want it, but not enough.

And Dick looked at him as they
shared a common stare,
and pulled the chamber back, sending
the .45 caliber round out
of the side, bouncing off
the boy's head, and landing
on the floor as he put the
pistol back down and lifted
another bottle,
knowing that that bullet
wasn't going anywhere.

A Christmas poem. During this time I was on a temporary assignment as a police officer on Camp Lejeune. I would go to a post, usually alone, for twelve hours, not including a PT session, brief, and debrief. Coming back to North Carolina, I had a miserable outbreak of eczema that engulfed my entire body. One marine said I looked like a leper. The doctor prescribed me a steroid cream, but taking such a large dose made my skin worse and also deepened my depression. As gas prices were ascending faster than my salary, there was some stress, but it was nothing compared to the emotional turmoil I faced between the combination of poison and pain my body was enduring. My wife later told me that I would regularly jump out bed in the middle of the night (or day when I was working nights) and search and clear the whole house. One day I ran outside, grabbed my youngest, and ran back inside as though saving her from some great danger. I have no recollection of these events. As I would drive home, I would talk to myself, which is not unusual, but it was violently angry, and there were many days that I wished I was dead.

Falling Down

Cloudy day today
and I'm here
forcing the words
because it's seven days
'til payday
and I've got eleven bucks
in the bank,
twelve cents in my pocket,
and two kids at home
as the gas tank in my car

cruises on E for as long
as it can. I pull into
a gas station, open the trunk,
check the seats, under the
mats for loose change or some
magical dollar that went
unnoticed, finding nothing.
I've done this before.

The ashtray is full of
sticky pennies from a soda
a year before.
How many sodas have I
bought since then? I wonder.
Surely enough for a full
tank of gas.
People pretend not to
know why they're
stressed out when their
kids' feet are too big for the
shoes they're in, or the legs
too long for the pajamas
grandma and grandpa bought on
their last visit.
Well, I do.

I dig the pennies out
(a big handful) and
walk into the store like
I don't have problems,
just a fistful of filth,
and go into the bathroom
to find good fortune as
I dump the pennies in
the soapy water. A dime
and two nickels.
The lady behind the counter

looks at me as though I
should be embarrassed to
buy $0.88 worth of gas, but
I don't have time for
that.

I get home tired and
break down in the driveway
crying uncontrollably, knowing
that I'm falling down
as my wife pulls me out
of bed at 5AM, dresses me,
and gets me out the door
each morning
with the lunch she made
an hour before, and into the
car she de-iced ten minutes ago.

I get to work on time –
most times – load
my Beretta and sit
waiting for the day to start,
wanting to kill myself,
telling other Marines, but
telling them it's just the
steroids the doctor gave me
to kill the pain, not
something I've always wanted.
8PM: I'm home.
K puts the girls to bed
and I get mad at her that
she let Claudia open one
of the presents under the
tree while she cooks me
dinner. It's Christmas,
but I had to work so
we're waiting.

I load the dishwasher and
sit down to write with
no paper so I tear whatever
blank pages I can find out
of the back of the books
I own and get three
to four hundred more words
into a book called Mission 10,
my fourth unpublished novel,
and lay down sometime between
ten and twelve, kiss my
wife, hear the baby cry
and roll over as she gets
her, then wakes me
again at five.

I get to work and
wonder,
how is it going to end,
as I put another round
into the chamber and
walk into another day.

COMING home is a war in itself. We would witness the struggles of other families as returning marines would lose control of their tempers – myself included – almost always exclusively with their children. Feelings of violence are very regularly beneath the surface after an extended period of time in a warzone. This state is called hypervigilance. I had experienced it on at least three occasions that didn't involve me being abusive to my family. Once, when I was at the armory a waft of air that smelled like burning trash came across me briefly and I began vomiting. Another time, I was driving home and a paper bag was in the street. I swerved onto the sidewalk and almost hit a house as though avoiding an improvised explosive device (IED). And the last time was when I was at a friend's house watching someone play one of those war video games that took place in Fallujah. It was very accurate and the surround sound made me feel as though I was set up with a radio. As my heart raced, my friend peeked around a corner and shot a member of his own fire team, leading me to inform him that, 'THAT'S BLUE-ON-BLUE YOU FUCKING ASSHOLE!'

Upon coming home from Iraq, I had filled out the paperwork and gotten my recommendations to take the indoc to be a reconnaissance man, but after I returned, I had to contend with the reality that while it was very hard to be home again, and would have been easier to leave and join a special forces unit, volunteering further would have been the worst thing for my family.

Warfare

Signs say Daddy's Home,
Welcome Home,
Our Hero, and there's yelling through

the cul de sac.
"Do this, Billy and Jessica," he
says. When they don't, which they
won't, "I SAID DO IT!"
And I know how he feels as I look
through the almost washed away paint
from September into my house that
said WELCOME
    HOME
    DADDY
    WE LOVE
    YOU
that's now somewhere else never to
return to my door as both my neighbors
are gone. We sent them each a care
package saying 'don't die' as their
pregnant wives cry themselves to
sleep at night.

That guy's still yelling as I suspect
will be the boys who live next to
me, and I won't talk to them,
either.
What would I say?
I know how you feel.
Fuck that. No one
knows how you feel.

It's like when the Irish were freed
and the negroes were freed,
and freedom didn't make them rich.
Italy is in a state of elected
communism, and my school principal
relative had some influence in that.
The US is falling down. This war
—my war—was paid for
with a credit card by men who ought

to take a course in bookkeeping,
but won't.
Inflation has outpaced pay raises
every year I know since my Vice
President relative was in office
during the Great Depression;
but no one cares because we have
more conveniences than ever.

I walk around knowing these things,
knowing I'm alone, feeling as I
imagine some IRA man or a free
black boy who was born that way does
when I walk down the street,
waiting for someone to call me
a fucking pig, or a nigger,
so I can split his face open.
I walk around knowing these things,
and it's like being shot at on
a Sunday morning. Why weren't
they at church? Why wasn't I
at church? It could've saved
us all. They say only Jesus can
save us, but we have to choose
to be saved. He won't just pluck
us out of the damnation we call
worship. We need the son when
we crave the Father. And I
crave him like nothing else.
I scream, "God where are you?
I need you."
I do.
I need Him like the wife He gave
me, and I'm grateful for every day
as well as our daughters, but live
in hunger, refusing to feed myself,
because off in the distance

I hear something.

The bell tolls.
It tolls and tolls.
There's ringing across the land.
I grab my gun, ignore the One;
it's time for war.

untitled

The words trot across the page
as I try not to over think them.
It's another year – New Year's Day – and
K takes down our Christmas
decorations. 27 minutes ago we
could hear the neighbors:

10, 9, 8...HAPPY NEW YEAR!
Pop-pop go the Roman Candles and
other things that men like me sell to
everyone else when they prepare for
Super Bowl Sunday, The Orange Bowl,
and whatever else it is that they do.

5 hours ago we were leaving Wal-mart
with a gallon of milk and some plaster
while a mother doing her last minute shopping
for the champagne that replaces
beer tonight, snatched up her 1-year-old
and told her she was going to
"rip it up."
Last night it was the cowboy with
his big belt buckle that slapped his
2-year-old in the ass as I waited for
her to move so I could get to
the register next to them.
"Git!" he said as the cashier rang up
his many 20 oz. Mountain Dews
and her dress (no jacket) fit
like a shirt as her 1-year-old
brother was "fit for a spankin'" while
a fetus lay in momma. Belt-Buckle-
Billy offered to trade his two for mine;
they said they had five, and we offered
to just take theirs. No dice.

12:40

The neighbors are standing around.
Now what?
Not much.

Another year.
Another novel.
Another war – the war at home. They
call it homecoming, but it's a trench
full of Agent Orange and we're Chinese
Generals who tried to win in Vietnam,
Legionnaires who tried to win in
Vietnam, Americans from
Desert Storm, saddened by the lack
of killing and guilty for our desire.

It's one Christmas to the next and
it's these kids that keep me anchored
away from the edge. They bring me home
for a hug and a kiss and the solace
that used to be at the bottom of a
bottle, but the bottles are all gone now.

We fought off food stamps and found
that in Orlando there are neighborhoods
for those who own Disney World and
projects for those who work there, and
they're only an exit apart – like everything
in this life – and all the yuppie parents
and snob kids I grew up with can't see
the trailer park for the trees. But now
I'm just over-thinking the words and
have to put this away because it's 1:15,
and the girls will be up in 6 hours.

AT this point, a year has almost passed from when I wrote "Falling Down." My time in the Marine Corps is coming to an end. I'm a Platoon Sergeant in charge of a logistics office and I also perform safety inspections on buildings, as well as accident investigations. Not too long after this, I was taken out of the rotation of Sergeant of the Guard and placed into that of Officer of the Day, which is almost exclusively reserved for staff NCOs and officers.

During this time, I am continuously working to get a book published—to get anything published—but cannot seem to do so, and realize that I may have to stay in the Corps for the simple fact that I've never done anything else that I was good at that paid a regular salary. What little money I did have I had wasted on bad investments in the stock market and self-publishing a short novel that was nothing more than a poor version of *Post Office*.

untitled

It's a late Sunday night, a week
before the Super Bowl.
Last year I was on traffic duty;
now I'm babysitting at the barracks,
doing my tours, seeing shoes in the
trees with a mop and whatever else.
There's trash outside the rooms of
plastic wrappers and imperfect
beer cans.

Something just happened in the
football match and I hear DID
YOU SEE THAT SHIT!

Could be good or bad, and
probably is.

And I'm here because this is the
only thing I'm good at. My best
writing is the most recent, and
recently it's been to agents (99 this
year; 93 last) and it's not good
enough to get them to look at
any of the stuff I wrote.

These days are sad when I realize
I'll be on the dole (they call them
unemployment benefits) at the end of
this contract as I take my girls
to the toy store and they want
everything.
For your birthday, I say,
but birthdays come faster than my
paternal talent, and we go to the
grocery store, and then through a new
housing development of castles half
a story taller and three times as
wide as ours on the base, and I hear,
Daddy, are we gonna buy this house?
No, honey
Why not?
Because I can't even buy you a dress
at the toy store.

And the next question is *why* as it
always is lately.

Why why why?

And I know why
as this poem ends, is

revised, ends, revised...

but I don't know how to tell
her in a way that will satisfy
the question.

I send another letter; this one
to a contest, and I realize that
I'm just going door to door again
like when I was a kid with a shovel
after a heavy snowstorm, or as a
college dropout with mortgage refinance
rates, and, now, with these things I make.
And that's what they are – things.

After the snowstorm, as a kid,
10, 11, 12-years-old, I guaranteed my
work. The mortgages were in the
hands of bankers. And these things
are nothing more than dirt on the
faded print of bad news.
A bird lands on the paper, flies
off, lays one on someone or some
thing, and the dirt departs somewhere
that we'll never see as it sets
and fades against an orange sky
as present as my hand to the page,
and as common as the talent I possess.

WITH the passage of time, we begin to heal. I cannot recall anything specific that led to me feeling better. At this time I was conducting accident investigations and giving instruction in such areas as Law of War and Code of Conduct (usually reserved for attorneys) and became well known in the battalion. As a result, marines came to talk to me about their time in. As we did, I was getting the therapy I needed. This poem references the year I spent at Niagara University from 2000-2001. A senior had invited me to join the poetry club, and I would go to the meetings to be with her. The poetry was typically sub-par, but the people were nice; nicer than I was.

A Taste of Sunshine

I remember those poet-kids from
that year in college.
They formed a nice circle
of verbal masturbation
and camaraderie.

There was Jenn, the little
red haired girl who'd invited
me; a nice young virgin about
to graduate. She'd find me
in the study lounge or my
dorm room, invite me to meetings
for the poetry club where
they all thought they were saying
so much when all they were
doing was swinging their tiny
peckers by way of their
little love poems, or whatever

it was that they'd had.

I never touched her but for one
night before Christmas playing a
game at one of the poet-kids'
house. It was
   right hand—blue
and we'd interlock arms with a
shove, and
   left leg—yellow
repeat the last.

We left that house
and she asked me with a hesitation
quelled only by years of waiting,
do you think I'm attractive,
and she dropped me off at my
dorm still a virgin, and better
off as her husband was
the only one to ever have her
while I went to my desk where
I kept the poem she gave me with
elegantly penned words
that were drenched in sexuality.

As these years pass I can
see that I'd trade the two
I'd had before for her.
It wouldn't be an even trade;
Big Head and The Whore for Jenn,
but the offer's out there
lingering in this place like
the fistful of sunshine I
snatched up as it fell from
the sky into my hand on
my way home yesterday.
I arrived, walking in the

door to hear some version
of 'daddy' exulted from my
littlest girl, and she ran to me,
crashing her face into my legs;
so happy.

I bent down with my fingers
still folded over it and opened
my hand to show her what I had.
And as quickly as it had
come she bent down
and ate it.
It disappeared from my
hand to the golden tendrils
of her hair, to her belly,
and her soul.
And the sorrow of this war
        disappeared.

THE following is based on a true story from a marine who was there.

Burial Ground

Some years ago there was a
mudslide in the Philippines.

During this time marines out of
Okinawa, Japan were on a ship
setting sail from Thailand
receiving mission orders hours
later; the mudslide...buried
school...imminent death.

The grunts and engineers hit the
shore with their tools ready to
go with ideas of rescuing these
children who had no hope save for
                    them.
Among them Lance Corporal
Hinkley brought up the first of the
treasure as his hand touched
another and he rushed to pull the
rocks off, seeing there was nothing
there but an indistinguishable
face among the wreckage. The
litter crew took the body and
he found another who was
just as well without him, and
plenty more before his shift

was called to break. Somewhere
in the distance below and beyond
he saw them sitting in the darkness,
waiting as they expired.

They entrenched for days, finding
their only glory to be in Thailand
where Hinkley had been sitting on
the beach with a beer in his
hand and a bitch at his
feet for three dollars, and
before that in Korea where
they cleared the DMZ and
partied with the ROC Marines
while the enemy to the north
never wavered.

Then they were on their ship again
and none of it meant anything anymore.
The stink of the death and the
mud and soulless bodies relieved of their
pain were left there to be uncovered
by young men like Hinkley and
Ross and Cole for no benefit but
the nightmares that have brought
their lives to a nearer end.

And somewhere beneath the mud
there is still a school.
The teachers give their lessons.
The children sit quietly
at their desks. And the lights switch
on and off with the opening
and closing of each day.
But mostly they wait,
and their waiting never ends.

I had started going to college again before I got out of the military, but had somehow convinced myself before this that I wasn't really in college; I was just escaping work by taking advantage of classes offered during the day. When the summer semester arrived, I realized that I was right back where I had left off seven years before. Working all this time had not propelled me ahead in any way, and now I had to go back to the institution of education that I was still convinced was pointless, but couldn't deny myself because the Montgomery GI Bill paid more than community college tuition, allowing me to keep the difference. Also, I had to realize that with this being my best option, there was no way around seeing what I had really made of myself by this point, which wasn't much.

Amateur Hour

I'm driving home from one more scheme of mine,
this one on sapping a government pension:
the GI Bill where GIs like me pay $1,800 to
Uncle Sam in exchange for $32,000 minus
community college tuition.
A week from now I'll be in the throes of British
literature and concocting fake papers on how and
why I have learned to appreciate art.

But it's the drive on this highway that's killing me
as I pull behind a car that says 'if you're gonna
ride my ass, at least pull my hair.'
It's amateur hour every hour out here
where I can also find that 'meat is murder,' and
that this other guy misses his ex, but his aim is
getting better.

These are people who want to acid-rain upon you
their unsolicited editorial commentary but don't have
the capacity to compile enough of it into a
book – much like this one. So they drive their cars and
slap their message of hope on the tail-ass of their motors
telling us that mean people suck, Jesus is a fish, Darwin is
a turtle, and that there's a bigger fish called
Truth that *loves* to eat turtles.

It's like watching girls play sports or me on the
Internet trying to find out what a labia is, only
to find that there are two of them with no information
on whether either one is worth a damn.
And it's no wonder I can't find the clitoris; it's
cloaked in a hood, peering out, laughing at me
while I try to draw the alphabet with my tongue
shortly before telling her that she doesn't have to
stop me so quickly all the time, because I can go all night.

And that's what she's afraid of.

THERE'S a Vietnam era song by this same title. Hearing it, I felt like someone really understood how I felt and had put it into words when I could not. As I mentioned in the opening pages, I was a patriot, and my belief in, and loyalty to, those who led me into a war blinded me to the point that I entered with no foresight of what was to come, and then no comprehension of exactly what I had seen. Of everything I could figure, I came to realize I was part of the problem. Because of me, there was a war, or, at least, a continuance of it. For this, I bear at least some responsibility.

Universal Soldier

I was born into this world frustrated,
ignorant of what it was on that early
March morning,
choking to death on the very thing
that gave me life.
Everything I would do
I would do the hard way.

As the early trials of Spring became Summer
I became a universal soldier
who could stand on my own
or in the presence of any other,
making his absence unrecognizable.

Without me, there would be no wars.
I was a universal soldier,
a single unit of dictatorial capital
for the utility of rare men.
I trained, received pay, gained promotion,

and left for a war that needed me.

And when I came home, I came home as
nothing, knowing that I always would be
and that nothing in this life would satisfy me.
For I had been a universal soldier.

THIS last poem was written four years later. It was on Memorial Day, 2012. I was working as an accountant during the week and doing security for a wealthy family on the weekends. Part of my job was to make sure that no boaters came up on the private beach (about a mile of it). As I drove the ATV up and down the coast of the Long Island Sound I would see dozens of horseshoe crabs. As I did this, I knew that I could step on one, and there was nothing that would be done about it. I could walk off leaving the crab to suffer until a seagull took it for easy pickings as the bird devoured it while it still breathed. To do this with no conscience, and perhaps even some joy, I would have had to have thought of them as *things* as opposed to being alive. Taking the steps to realize this, and having met some people through both of my lines of work who were very wealthy, I also realized that as I was "a single unit of capital," as noted in the previous poem, I was also nothing more than a thing to them when they sent me to war. They didn't know anything about me, nor did they care, but I believed in them so much; I believed in them as though they loved me, and would never hurt me. And for this I was willing to kill and die, which led to an extreme desire for the latter when I was finished with what they had me do, but they could not have cared less about me because I was not alive. To them, I was static; a thing that was part of their recorded data that would not be missed, but could possibly be capitalized on further if I had killed and/or died to their satisfaction.

Memorial Day

A light breeze comes in off the coast
gently gusting as the rocky sand gives
way with each step while the water laps

in as gently as the gusting breeze,
leading one to believe that all must
surely be in harmony.

And then I crush a horseshoe crab
under the blow of my bare foot for
no other reason than that she is weak
and I am strong.

Fifty paces out I see a couple coming
toward me, holding hands, and we smile and
wave at each other. Then they see my
shirt that says USMC and say
Happy Memorial Day
and move on never to be seen again
like those who this day is for.

Happy Memorial Day.
I can't find anything happy about it.
We were all true believers who
thought that surely the son of multi
generations of wealth and power
wouldn't fuck us so hard and
skillfully simply for his own amusement
just because we were weak
and he was strong.

But he did, and we loved it.
As we approached our climax, he
pulled off his red, white, and blue
condom, unsheathing Old Glory,
and discarding such colors, and being
such lovers we loved him more
for it as we could feel his pleasure,
and we desired to please him.

Then, right as he came—with us

only a half-step behind—he whispered
in our ear
I have AIDS
and he does have AIDS. That's what
this war is, our AIDS virus, and
it claims us a few at a time with
every interval, leaving our bodies
strewn about by the thousands
to be assembled in a line of
flag draped coffins well known
to be pauper's graves.

In the wake of our destruction is
the debris of all the widows
and widowers and half orphaned children
who love us all so much,
but all they are left with are
the memories painted brighter by our
absence, making us more than we
ever were, and misleading them as
we were misled.

And just as our belief and fire
and passion brought us to our
destruction, their way is doomed to
follow ours, and they, too,
will have AIDS.

Happy Memorial Day.

Afterword

I was a patriot. Whatever semblance of patriotism hadn't corroded away was stripped bare. I was no longer a patriot. I was so much more. I was a Marine.

The Author

CHRISTOPHER Pascale served in the US Marine Corps from 2003-2008 as a combat engineer. He currently lives on Long Island.

www.ingramcontent.com/pod-product-compliance
Lightning Source LLC
Chambersburg PA
CBHW060131050426
42448CB00010B/2064